Black Heroes of
the American Revolution

ODYSSEY

Black Heroes
of the American Revolution

BURKE DAVIS

Foreword by Edward W. Brooke

An Odyssey Book
Harcourt Brace & Company
San Diego   New York   London

Requests for permission to make copies of any
part of the work should be mailed to:
Permissions Department, Harcourt Brace & Company,
6277 Sea Harbor Drive, Orlando, Florida 32887-6777.

Library of Congress Cataloging-in-Publication Data
Davis, Burke, 1913–
Black heroes of the American Revolution: with prints and portraits of the
period/Burke Davis; foreword by Edward W. Brooke.
p.   cm.
"An Odyssey Book."
Includes bibliographical references and index.
Summary: An account of the black soldiers, sailors, spies, scouts, guides,
and wagoners who participated and sacrificed in the struggle for American
independence.
ISBN 0-15-208561-0 pb
1. United States—History—Revolution, 1775–1783—Afro-Americans—
Juvenile literature. 2. Afro-Americans—Biography—Juvenile literature.
[1. Afro-Americans—Biography. 2. United States—History—Revolution,
1775–1783—Afro-Americans.] I. Title.
E269.N3D383   1992
973.3′092′2—dc20   91-8921
[B]

Printed in the United States of America
I H G F E D

To Tammy Roberts

FOREWORD

Burke Davis, in and on the pages that follow, casts a bright beam of light on an aspect of the American Revolution that has, for too long, been steeped in shadow or darkness.

That stage of our history has always been populated and dominated by George Washington, Paul Revere, General Lafayette, Ethan Allen, Benjamin Franklin, and a score or two of other authentic heroes whose courage, deeds of glory, grit and perseverance finally brought freedom and a new, free nation into being.

But there were other heroes. Men whose names have never found their way into the traditional history books and so into the classrooms of our country and thus, eventually and finally, into the consciousness of Americans—young and old.

Most of *these* heroes should have entered the struggle for freedom with a lingering doubt. They, after all, were slaves—the property of others. Why should they fight for liberty—for independence—for freedom?

Liberty, independence, freedom for whom?

If there were doubts, they were dowsed and drowned by the belief that the Revolution was a path to freedom for all women and men—that the Revolution was a vital, first step toward equality for blacks in the new world.

These black American Revolutionary heroes gambled on and for the future. They read and knew the words of Patrick Henry. They were caught up and possessed by the fever and fervor of freedom.

And so, they went to work. Burke Davis tells you who they were—what they did—how they helped to forge and foster the United States of America.

Their deeds will make you proud. Even more important, their commitment to the dream that was to become our country, to brotherhood and to a *United* States of America is a lesson we must never forget.

Edward W. Brooke
UNITED STATES SENATE
1967–1979

CONTENTS

Black Heroes of
the American Revolution

1

The Histories Were White

White histories have remembered white heroes and have recorded little or nothing of the thousands of black men who played an important part in the American Revolution. Yet at least five thousand black men served on the patriot side during the seven-year Revolution. Perhaps it is not strange that these black fighting men were forgotten since the earlier Continental Congress that adopted the Declaration of Independence struck out Thomas Jefferson's angry words that condemned the slave trade. When the white Congress spoke of "all men" as free and equal, it did not include black men.

The names of some black war heroes who *had* been honored for their bravery were later removed from monuments and history books in the years after the war. But most black men who fought in the Revolution left no record of their experiences because most of them were slaves and few of them could read and write. Under the laws of most states slaves could not be educated.

When the Revolution began, only two and one-half million people lived in the American colonies, half a million of them black. Only a few of the blacks had been freed—the rest of them were slaves. By the end of the war, about 60,000 slaves had been set free, many because they had helped to win the nation's freedom, many because their contributions helped to pass laws in the Northern states to abolish slavery shortly after the war.

Luckily, even though the feats of most black soldiers were not recorded, we know of some who fought bravely in this white man's war.

One who helped to save the stories of black heroes for later Americans was the famous white poet John Greenleaf Whittier, who wrote many years after the Revolution that the service of black men should no longer be "carefully kept out of sight." He praised the "founding fathers" who were black: "They have had no historian. With here and there an exception, they all passed away. . . . Yet enough is known to show that the free colored men of the United States bore their full proportion of the sacrifices and trials of the Revolutionary war."

WILLIAM LEE, whose name is unknown to most Americans, was by the side of George Washington at almost every minute of the Revolution, sharing dangers, victories, and defeats and was perhaps the general's closest companion before and after the war. Washington later gave William Lee his freedom and left money to care for him in old age. It was probably because of his friendship with his black companion that the general, even though, like Jefferson, a slaveholder, said that there was "not a man living" who wished more sincerely than he that slavery could be abolished by law.

Another black man who fought throughout the war was OLIVER CROMWELL of Burlington, New Jersey. On a spring day in 1852, a newspaper reporter stopped before Cromwell's small house on East Union Street. Cromwell was then a thin, white-haired man whose hands trembled with age. Few of Burlington's people, black or white, realized that old Oliver Cromwell was one of the last living soldiers of the Revolution. The final battle of the war had been fought seventy-one years before.

When the reporter asked his age, Cromwell said, "I'm very old. I'm one hundred years old today."

The veteran's memory was still clear. He recalled enlisting as a private in the Second New Jersey Regiment, commanded by the enormously fat Colonel Israel Shreve. He remembered the long retreat before the British from New York, down through New Jersey and into Pennsylvania. He remembered the crossing of the Delaware in the attack on Trenton and the second surprise American victory a few days later at Princeton, where Washington's little army "knocked the British about lively."

Cromwell remembered most of the great battles fought by Washington, especially Brandywine and Monmouth, near Philadelphia, and the final victory at Yorktown, where he saw the fall of the last American killed in battle.

To prove his service, the old man proudly showed a discharge signed by Washington in June, 1783, after Cromwell had served more than six years in the New Jersey battalion. The discharge proved that Oliver had won the Badge of Merit for his long and faithful service—he had enlisted for the duration of the war, at a time when thousands of white Americans refused to enlist at all and when others marched away from the army's camp at the end of their short terms regardless of the country's danger.

Oliver Cromwell died in January, 1853. But though he left behind several children, grandchildren, and great-grandchildren, there was no one to raise a marker over the grave of the private who had fought so long for his country, with so little hope of reward. There were few to remember that this brave man had volunteered for the American army when he was a twenty-year-old farm boy and that he had endured all the sufferings of defeat and retreat and the winters at Valley Forge and Morristown to take part in the last act at Yorktown.

GEORGE LATCHOM was the hero of a short skirmish in Virginia. During the last months of fighting in the Revolution, in 1781, a small British army landed on a sandy shore called Henry's Point, within a few miles of Yorktown. There were no troops of the regular American army to meet these invaders, but there was a band of Virginians, home guard soldiers who were known as militia.

A few of these untrained troops, led by Colonel John Cropper, fired at the British as they moved from their boats to the shore and kept up the fire until the redcoats were only a few yards away, charging with their bayonets. The white Colonel Cropper stood far in front of his men, exchanging shots with the British until the last. By his side was only one man: the slave George Latchom, who was owned by one of Cropper's neighbors.

Cropper and Latchom retreated through a marsh, where the colonel sank to the waist in soft mud, helpless before the oncoming enemy. George Latchom shot and killed the nearest redcoat, and when other enemy soldiers hesitated, he grabbed Cropper beneath the arms, tugged him free, and carried him to safety across the marsh. Men of both armies marveled at Latchom's strength, for Colonel Cropper was a large man who weighed some two hundred pounds.

As soon as the militia band was out of danger, Colonel Cropper bought George Latchom from his owner, set him free, and, as the colonel's biographer wrote, "befriended him in every way he could, as an evidence of his gratitude, till Latchom's death."

The battle of Brandywine, in Pennsylvania, saw many black soldiers in Washington's ranks, none of them braver or more patriotic than the artilleryman EDWARD HECTOR.

Sir William Howe, at the head of an army of some 17,000 British and German soldiers, marched against Philadelphia in the late summer of 1777. To meet this danger to the capital, General Washington placed his army along Brandywine Creek, made headquarters at a crossing known as Chad's Ford, and on a wooded hillside nearby placed his cannon. Among those who waited with the big guns was the thirty-three-year-old private Edward Hector of the Third Pennsylvania Artillery.

Hector and his companions had a long wait. The enemy appeared early in the morning of September 11, but the British did not try to cross the stream. Instead, Sir William Howe led most of his army on a surprise march far up the bank of Brandywine Creek to a hidden crossing in the woods and, within a few hours, had circled into the rear of the American army.

Washington sent many of his troops hurrying to the flank and rear to meet the oncoming redcoats and soon galloped through the woods and across fields on horseback, leaping fences in his way. It was too late. The roar of battle told the general that the British had struck with great strength. The new American lines could not be held, though his troops fought with great bravery. A few men began to flee, and then hundreds ran off the field in panic. The rear of the American army was protected by a few hundred men who held off the redcoat columns until dark. Washington's men retreated in confusion.

During the fighting on the flank, British and German troops who had been left at Chad's Ford began firing heavily across the Brandywine, and when the roar of the main battle was at its peak, the invaders splashed across the stream and stormed up the hill in the face of American musket and cannon fire.

Edward Hector's artillery battery poured shot and shell into the enemy ranks until the charging redcoats were among the guns. Americans then began to flee, leaving guns, ammunition, horses, and wagons to the British.

But even now, when the chance of victory was gone, some of Washington's men refused to give up. One of these was Edward Hector. When he was ordered to abandon the ammunition wagon he had driven to the field, Private Hector shouted, "Never! I'll save my horses or die myself!" While most men of the army scurried to the rear, Hector saved his wagon. As a Norristown, Pennsylvania, newspaper said, "He instantly started on his way, and . . . amid the confusion . . . he calmly gathered up . . . a few stands of arms which had been left on the field by the retreating soldiers, and safely retired with wagon, team and all, in the face of the victorious foe."

The next day, when Washington had pulled together his regiments and marched them off in good order to fight another day, Edward Hector's full wagon of ammunition rolled with the Third Pennsylvania Artillery as usual.

This veteran's reward for his faithful service was not soon in coming. In his old age, when some of his Norristown neighbors tried to have an army pension paid to him, they were refused.

It was only when he was near death in 1834, at the age of ninety, that the legislature of Pennsylvania voted a reward to Edward Hector. The reward was $40, the only payment he ever had for his army services.

It was little more than enough to bury the brave wagoner of Brandywine.

AUSTIN DABNEY, a slave on a Georgia plantation, was given a chance to win his freedom by serving in the American army when his master was drafted and asked Austin to take his place.

The slave accepted and soon became an artilleryman in the Georgia corps commanded by Colonel Elijah Clark. These gunners fought in several battles against the British in the South, including one at Cowpens, South Carolina, where almost an entire redcoat army was killed, wounded, or captured.

Austin Dabney and his companions also fought at the little battle of Kettle Creek, "the hardest ever fought in Georgia." Dabney was shot in the thigh during this heavy fighting. Later the Governor of Georgia said of Austin, "No soldier under Clark was

braver, or did better service during the Revolutionary struggle."

Dabney was unable to walk for a time after being
wounded at Kettle Creek, but was nursed back to
health by a white soldier named Harris. Austin Dabney was so grateful that he spent several years working for the Harris family and insisted on sending
the eldest son of his rescuer through college from
his own pocket.

Dabney drew a pension like other veterans of
the Revolution, but in 1819, when old soldiers were
given chances in a lottery for lands in the western
part of the state, he was not allowed to take part.
Soon afterward, when the Georgia legislature finally
awarded him 112 acres for his "bravery and forti-
tude" in several battles, Dabney's white neighbors
in Madison County protested, claiming that it was
"an indignity" to white men to have the black veteran treated equally in the awarding of public lands.

But Austin Dabney was not to be defeated. Not
only did he win his land grant, he also eventually
became a close friend of several wealthy planters of
his neighborhood. He owned fine horses and took
them to racetracks, where they ran against the horses
of his white friends.

Dabney spent his old age in the village of Dan-
ielsville, Georgia, where he often went into the judge's

chambers after the adjournment of the county court, talking with lawyers and judges about the long-gone days of the Revolution. With admiration one of them said of him: "His memory was retentive, his understanding good, and he described what he knew well."

Among the several black soldiers who fought at the battle of Bunker Hill was SALEM POOR, a freeman who had enlisted in Andover, Massachusetts, in the company of Captain Benjamin Ames. Few whites had ever heard of the twenty-eight-year-old Private Poor before he left his wife behind and marched to the siege of Boston, but he became famous in Massachusetts immediately after the battle. Poor is believed to have shot and killed a leader of the British attack, Lieutenant Colonel James Abercrombie.

Fourteen American officers were so proud of Salem Poor's bravery at Bunker Hill that they asked Congress to reward the "great and Distinguished" black soldier. The American commander, Colonel William Prescott, was among those who signed this petition: "Wee declare that A Negro Man Called Salem Poor of Col. Fryes Regiment. Capt. Ames. Company in the late Battle at Charleston, behaved like an Experienced Officer, as Well as an Excellent Soldier, to Set forth Particulars of his Conduct would be Tedious, Wee Would Only begg leave to say in the Person of this sd. [said] Negro Centers a Brave & gallant Soldier."

But though Salem Poor remained in the army for many years and fought at the battle of White Plains, New York, and lived through the bitter winter camp at Valley Forge, there is no record that Congress ever voted him a reward.

2

Eight Invisible Men

There were also black men in Washington's ranks who became well known in their day as brave soldiers and sailors—and were still doomed to be forgotten by later Americans. Among those heroes who were highly praised were eight who served their country in many different ways.

The first of these men fought in the opening battles of the Revolution, in the villages of Concord and Lexington, Massachusetts. He was, in fact, only one of several black soldiers among the American Minutemen who fired "the shots heard round the world."

When a British column reached Lexington, where they planned to seize powder and weapons stored by the patriots, the redcoats were faced by a small band of Americans drawn up on the village green.

Major John Pitcairn, the British commander, ordered the rebels to scatter and go to their homes and opened fire when they refused. Among those who returned fire against Pitcairn's men was PETER SALEM, a slave who had marched in from the nearby town of Framingham as a private in the company of Captain Simon Edgel. Salem was armed with a flint-lock musket, like most other patriot soldiers on the green, and he fired and loaded through the brief fight until Major Pitcairn called for a retreat and the British marched back toward their base in Boston.

Peter Salem probably followed the redcoats with his companions, who kept up a hot fire from behind walls, fences, and trees, sniping at the British until they reached the safety of the city. It is certain that one of the last Americans wounded on this day in April, 1775, was a black man, shot as he fired with others from a house near Back Bay, where the redcoats climbed into boats and were rowed into Boston.

Two months later, when an American army had gathered outside Boston to pen the British in the city, Peter Salem was again among the more than twenty black patriots ready for battle.

The rebels fortified hills overlooking Boston one night, and the next day, when the British advanced to attack in the battle known as Bunker Hill, Major Pitcairn met Peter Salem once again. The meeting cost the officer his life.

Salem "took aim at Major Pitcairn, as he was rallying the . . . British troops, & shot him thro the head. . . ." The major fell dead just as he was shouting to his men, "The day is ours."

Soon afterward, white soldiers of the New England army raised money to reward Peter Salem for his bravery, and the black hero was presented to General Washington as the man who had killed Pitcairn.

Salem remained in the army for several years, long enough to fight in the bloody battles of Saratoga and Stony Point.

After the war he settled in Leicester, Massachusetts, where he barely earned a living weaving cane seats for chairs. He died in the poorhouse in Framingham in 1816. Almost seventy years later, citizens of the town erected a monument to Peter Salem's memory.

One of the most famous paintings of the Revolution shows George Washington in a crowded small boat, crossing the icy Delaware River on Christmas night, 1776. The general was leading his tiny army across the river in a surprise attack on Trenton, New Jersey.

In the boat, helping to row through the ice floes, was PRINCE WHIPPLE, a slave who was the bodyguard of General William Whipple of New Hampshire. The tall black man may have been the first to step ashore when Washington's boat landed on the dark banks, and he was certainly near the general during the night and early morning as the patriots marched through snow and sleet to attack the sleeping German troops in Trenton. No one remembered this bodyguard's part in the nine-mile march against Trenton, but it was never forgotten that he was one of the leaders in the general's dangerous crossing of the river.

Prince Whipple was born in the African village of Amabou, where he lived until he was ten years old. His father, who was a man of some wealth, then sent the boy with one of his young cousins to America, where they were to be educated. But when they arrived in America, a greedy ship's captain took the boys to Baltimore, where he sold them into slavery.

Prince was bought by William Whipple and taken to Portsmouth, New Hampshire, where he lived as a servant until the Revolution. After the war, in which his master served General Washington as an aide and became a general, Prince Whipple was given his freedom for his faithful service—but this was only after he, joined by about twenty other black men in Portsmouth, had written the legislature of New Hampshire to protest that they had been born as free men in Africa and that, as the Declaration of Independence had told the world, "freedom is an inherent right" of all men and could not be taken away by force. Slavery, these black patriots declared, was hateful to all men who cared for "the equal dignity of human nature." It is not known how soon after this petition that he was freed from slavery, but it must have been only a few months.

This black bodyguard was so highly trusted by General Whipple that he was once sent with a large sum of money from Salem, Massachusetts, to Portsmouth. When two robbers attacked him on the road, near the town of Newburyport, Prince Whipple knocked down one of the highwaymen with the handle of a heavy whip and shot the other with a pistol, saving General Whipple's money.

Prince Whipple, "beloved by all who knew him," as an early historian said, died in New Hampshire not long after the Revolution, leaving behind a widow and several children to enjoy the freedom he had won for them.

On May 1, 1777, as the second year of the Revolution opened, eighteen-year-old AGRIPPA HULL enlisted as a private in General John Patterson's Massachusetts brigade. Hull, who was born free in Northampton, Massachusetts, had lived in Stockbridge since his boyhood. He signed up for the duration of the war and served for six years and two months, most of this time as orderly to the Polish nobleman General Thaddeus Kosciusko, Washington's chief engineer. In this service Hull survived such bloody battles as Saratoga, in upstate New York, and Eutaw Springs, in South Carolina. He did not leave the army until July, 1783, almost two years after Yorktown.

When the war was over, Hull settled down in Stockbridge, where he farmed a small plot and made a living from odd jobs. He married a fugitive slave and adopted another as his daughter. In his later years he was known by whites and blacks alike as the village seer, remarkable for his keen mind, his wisdom and biting wit.

One day when Hull went to hear a famous mulatto preacher in a Stockbridge church, he was asked by a vain and haughty white man, "Well, how do you like nigger preaching?"

"Sir," said Hull, "he was half black and half white. I liked *my* half. How did *you* like yours?"

Almost twenty years after the war, when General Kosciusko revisited the United States, Hull went to New York for an affectionate reunion with his old companion. During this visit to the country he had helped to liberate, the Polish general was awarded a tract of land in Ohio, which he sold to found a school for black Americans.

In 1828, when he was almost seventy years old and asked that his soldier's pension be mailed directly to his home, he was told to send in his discharge with this request. He did so reluctantly, for, he said, he would almost rather give up his pension than lose the discharge signed by General Washington.

Hull died almost twenty years later at the age of eighty-nine, and was remembered with respect by the people of his town. His portrait still hangs in the historical room of the Stockbridge library.

When Ethan Allen and his Green Mountain Boys from Vermont stormed the British at Fort Ticonderoga and captured valuable cannon, at least three of their men were black volunteers—LEMUEL HAYNES, Primas Black, and Epheram Blackman. Haynes, who was born in West Hartford, Connecticut, in 1753, fought in the war's northern campaigns, then returned to farming and married Elizabeth Babbit in 1778. He later became a famous preacher in Manchester, Vermont, and Granville, New York, and was the father of nine children, one of whom became a lawyer and another a physician. Haynes died in 1833 in Bennington, Vermont, where the town museum displays his portrait to this day.

Three black men from Virginia left behind them distinguished but brief records of their service in the Revolution. JOSEPH RANGER was a freeman who served in the Virginia Navy for nine years—until the little fleet was disbanded four years after the end of the Revolution. Ranger fought on the *Hero*, *Dragon*, *Jefferson*, and *Patriot* before his capture by the British on the eve of the battle of Yorktown. He was later awarded a grant of a hundred acres by the state of Virginia and a pension of $96 a year.

One of Ranger's companions was the slave CAESAR TARRANT, a pilot who was set free by the Virginia Assembly because of his bravery. Tarrant became a well-to-do citizen of Hampton, Virginia, after the war and left his daughter more than 2,600 acres in the Ohio Territory.

From nearby Portsmouth, young WILLIAM FLORA, a freeman who volunteered in Colonel William Woodford's First Virginia Regiment, marched with his unit to Great Bridge, near Norfolk, in December, 1775. When a British force charged, the last man to leave the bridge, still firing, was William Flora, who was praised by a newspaper of the day for holding his ground until "he had fired eight times; and after receiving a whole platoon, made his escape over the causeway into our breastwork."

Flora became a leading businessman of Portsmouth after the war as owner of a large livery stable and left a substantial estate to his heirs.

On September 6, 1781, while General Washington was leading the French and American armies into Virginia to trap Lord Cornwallis at Yorktown, a band of British soldiers sailed up the Thames River in Connecticut to burn the towns of Groton and New London. The redcoats were led by the American traitor Benedict Arnold.

Two men who saw the enemy boats put out for the shore were a white farmer named Latham and his black slave, LAMBERT LATHAM, who were tending cattle in a field. The two ran across the fields to join other Americans in a small earthwork called Fort Griswold, where a few cannon were ready to fire on the British raiders. The fort's commander was Lieutenant Colonel William Ledyard.

Arnold's men surrounded Ledyard's small fort, but though they fired steadily, the garrison refused to surrender. Lambert Latham had a painful bullet wound in the hand, but fought on beside his master, loading and firing his musket at the enemy again and again.

At last the larger redcoat force began climbing the walls of Fort Griswold. When many defenders had been killed, a British officer shouted, "Who commands this fort?"

"I once did," Colonel Ledyard said. "You do now." Ledyard handed over his sword to the redcoat officer—who at once ran the blade through Ledyard's body to the hilt.

Lambert Latham, who was standing by the commander, turned on the British officer furiously and stabbed him with his bayonet. Many British soldiers then slashed the slave with their bayonets until he died with thirty-three bayonet wounds in his body.

Latham fell, as a historian wrote, "nobly avenging the death of his commander."

More than fifty years later, when the state of Connecticut put up a marker in honor of the eighty-four patriots killed by the British raiders on that September day, the name of Colonel Ledyard was placed at the top, followed by the names of eighty-one other whites. At the bottom, under the heading "Colored Men," were the names of Latham and Freeman, two slaves, and to the disgust of his descendants, the name of the brave Lambert Latham, who had been known by the nickname of "Lambo," had been carved in marble as "Sambo."

3

Two Famous Patriots

When offered his freedom and a life of ease in England, the young black sailor from Philadelphia replied, "No, I'm a prisoner for my country, and I'll never be a traitor to her."

Just before the end of the Revolution, a fifteen-year-old black youth signed on as a powder boy aboard the American privateer *Royal Louis*, a small ship commanded by Stephen Decatur, Sr.

The youngster was JAMES FORTEN, who had been born free in Philadelphia, where he had attended the school of an anti-slavery Quaker. This slender young volunteer was to become one of the wealthiest men in Philadelphia after the war. He was already a war veteran, for he had served as a drummer in the army.

The *Royal Louis* put to sea to prey on British shipping, with the hope of dividing captured prizes among the officers and crew. Of her crew of two hundred, twenty were black. The first cruise was bloody but successful, and Captain Decatur's ship forced a British Navy brig to surrender. The second cruise ended in disaster. A heavily armed enemy frigate, the *Amphyon*, with the aid of two other warships, battered the *Royal Louis* so fiercely that Decatur was forced to surrender.

It was a bad moment for James Forten. The British seldom exchanged black prisoners who fell into their hands, but usually sold them in the West Indies to serve as plantation laborers under cruel overseers and the merciless tropical sun. But James Forten was one of the lucky prisoners aboard the *Amphyon*. He met the captain's son, a boy of his own age, and the two became friends at once. The English boy was so fond of the quick-witted black American, and so impressed by his skill at playing marbles, that he persuaded his father to offer Forten a life of ease in England. Forten refused, declaring he would not be a traitor to his country.

Rather than shipping him to the West Indies, the British captain sent Forten to the prison ship *Jersey*, which was anchored off Long Island. "Thus," James Forten wrote later, "did a game of marbles save me from a life of West Indian servitude."

There were days when Forten felt that he had not been so lucky after all, for he was shoved deep into the hold of the ship with a thousand other prisoners, forced to live on wormy meat, crusts of moldy bread and foul water, gasping for breath in the stinking, overcrowded quarters. Each day, fresh bodies were hauled out of the hold for burial in the sand dunes ashore. During the war more than 10,000 American prisoners died on the rotting hulk of this prison ship.

James Forten once had a chance to escape when a patriot officer, who was to be exchanged for a British prisoner, left the *Jersey* with his chest. Forten had planned to crawl into the officer's chest and be carried to freedom, but stood aside to allow a younger white boy to hide instead. Forten helped to carry the chest over the side of the ship into a waiting boat and watched his smaller companion escape.

After enduring seven months in the floating hell of the *Jersey*, James Forten was set free in an exchange of prisoners and walked to his home in Philadelphia. During the next fifty years of his life, Forten was to become one of the best-known men of his city. He began to make sails for ships and was soon the head of a business employing scores of people. James Forten became an inventor as well as a manufacturer, gave much of his wealth to aid poor and struggling blacks, and became a founder of the Abolition movement to help end American

2 5

slavery. Among his friends was the famous white orator William Lloyd Garrison, who befriended many of the country's blacks.

Garrison won Forten's heart in his early speeches attacking slavery when he said, "I never rise to address a colored audience, without feeling ashamed of my own color, ashamed of having been identified with a race of men who have done you so much injustice."

James Forten lived to see his sons and grandsons become leaders in the anti-slavery crusade, but never regretted the years he spent as a drummer, powder boy, and prisoner during the Revolution.

Still, as he said in 1830 when it appeared that black slavery would never be stamped out, the war he had fought in was an incomplete revolution, and the country faced a real crisis, "The spirit of Freedom is marching with rapid strides and causing tyrants to tremble; may America awake . . ."

The most famous of the black men who fought in the cause of the Revolution was killed by a British soldier during the Boston massacre in 1770, five years before the outbreak of the war. He became the first martyr of the American Revolution.

Fresh snow lay in Boston's icy streets on the night of March 5, 1770, but the sky had cleared after dark and a new moon hung overhead. A cold wind from the harbor swept the Boston Common and shook the tents of British soldiers, who had been camped there for five months.

The streets were noisy as redcoats moved about, followed by bands of shouting civilians. The small city of 15,000 was crowded by men and boys who had come in from the country and nearby towns to help drive out the 1,000 redcoats, just as if they were enemies. There were occasional scuffles, as there had been for weeks past. Soldiers jostled and cursed the people, who replied with hoots, curses, and insults. These soldiers were the first ever sent from England to America in peacetime, ordered to the city by King George III after the Massachusetts legislature had protested harsh new trade laws for the colonies.

Now and then the redcoats were pelted by snowballs from the darkness, hundreds of frozen chunks with small stones in the center. A fight broke out— no one seemed to know how it had begun—and church bells rang an alarm. People looked out from their houses, and many came into the streets, armed with swords, axes, pitchforks, or boards ripped from old buildings. The crowds grew more daring as they became larger.

A sentry by the name of Montgomery who stood

before the Customs House on King Street found himself surrounded by people after a young barber's helper yelled, "There's a redcoat who hasn't paid for having his hair dressed."

"Shut up!" Montgomery said.

The boy cursed, the soldier struck him on the head with his musket butt, and the barber's helper went yowling down the street holding his head.

The crowd pressed about the sentry, chanting, "Hang the redcoats! Drive 'em out!"

More church bells rang as the barber's boy returned to jeer and point at Montgomery. The crowd increased. Captain Thomas Preston, the officer of the day, called for the guard, and twelve soldiers hurried to the Customs House. The crowd was forced back a few feet by bayonets. The muskets, Captain Preston said, were not loaded.

At that moment, as the civilians hesitated before the glistening blades, a small mob rushed down a nearby hill, its men armed with clubs. The newcomers were led by a burly black man named CRISPUS ATTUCKS, who urged them on in a loud, fierce voice. People on the streets stepped aside as Attucks charged. As John Adams said, the giant's appearance "was enough to terrify any person."

The black leader had formed his men in Dock Square and led them down King Street (now State

Street), trotting at the head of his company, his broad shoulders hunched.

Attucks dashed within a few feet of the line of redcoats at the Customs House and waved over his head a heavy stick of firewood.

"Come on, bloodybacks!" he yelled. "Shoot if you dare! Damn you, we know you don't dare."

The soldiers began loading their muskets. A young white man in the crowd begged Captain Preston to take his men back to their tents, but the officer refused. A soldier yelled, "Damn them. If they bother me, I'll fire." The redcoats now held their muskets breast high, with fingers on the triggers.

Crispus Attucks still towered over the captain, swinging his stick of wood and calling to his companions, "We're not afraid of them! Knock 'em over. They dare not fire."

Beside him stood Samuel Gray, the owner of a rope factory, who had led an attack on some of the soldiers a few days before. Gray also shouted encouragement to the mob and said that the troops would not fire. A club sailed through the air, knocking aside a British musket. Suddenly a hail of snowballs, stones, clubs, and sticks fell among the redcoats. The crowd raised a shout that rang through the streets, but above it rang an Indian war whoop from Attucks, who grabbed a bayonet with one hand

and at the same moment clubbed a soldier with his stick.

The twelve muskets roared. Attucks fell with two bullets in his chest, the first one fired by the sentry Montgomery. Samuel Gray went down beside him.

Both men died on the spot, almost at the feet of the soldiers. Stray shots killed Jonas Caldwell, a sailor who was standing in the middle of the street, and two other whites, seventeen-year-old Samuel Maverick and Patrick Carr, both of whom fell as they were hurrying toward the scene. Six other civilians were wounded, but were to recover.

The crowd fled, leaving the bodies behind, but as it grew and became noisier, it swarmed through the streets until it met Governor Thomas Hutchinson.

The Governor calmed the people by speaking to them from the balcony of a building. He promised to arrest Captain Preston and his men and to have the troops moved out of the city. The people then drifted away and returned to their homes.

Strangely enough, the people of Boston knew almost nothing about Crispus Attucks, who was hailed as the first victim in the cause that was to become the American Revolution.

Though little is known of his early life, Crispus Attucks is thought to have been the son of an African

father and an Indian mother. The mother, who be-
longed to the Natick tribe, was probably descended
from John Attucks, a Christian convert who was
executed by early New England colonists because
he sided with his tribe during an Indian uprising
known as King Philip's War. ("Attuck" was the word
for "deer" in the Natick language.)

By the time he had grown to manhood, Crispus
was a slave, the property of William Brown of Framingham, Massachusetts. But even as a slave, young
Attucks was unusually independent. He became well
known in his home town as a trader of horses and
cattle, shrewd enough to deal with free white men.
But though he kept for himself the money he made,
Attucks was unable to buy his freedom from his
master—and he was fiercely determined to be free.

At last, in the autumn of 1750, he took the only
way to freedom that was open to him. He ran away.
Brown advertised in the *Boston Gazette* on October
2, 1750:

> *Ran away from his Master* William Brown of
> Framingham . . . *a Molatto Fellow, about 27
> years of Age. Named Crispas 6 feet two Inches
> high, short curl'd Hair, his knees nearer together
> than common: had on a light colour'd Bearskin
> Coat . . .*

But though Brown offered ten pounds as a reward, Attucks was never caught—nor was he heard from again in Massachusetts until the night, twenty years later, when he reappeared as the leader of the patriot mob on March 5, 1770. It is thought that Attucks may have spent his twenty years of freedom as a sailor, working on cargo ships that sailed to and from the West Indies, but this is not certain. He is also said to have sailed whaling ships off the New England coast.

The stranger who had appeared just in time to give the white mob the courageous leadership to attack the redcoats was praised by white revolutionaries as the bravest of the victims of the street fight.

As Thomas Jefferson said, the blood of Crispus Attucks nourished the tree of liberty. The humble slave, who had the courage to flee his master and make a new life on his own, had been among the first Americans to die for the nation's liberty.

Three days later, a public funeral was held for the victims of the street battle. All shops in the city were closed and thousands of people flocked in from the nearby countryside. The *Boston Gazette* reported that the funeral was attended by the largest crowd ever assembled in North America.

The bodies of Attucks and Caldwell, which had

lain in their coffins at Faneuil Hall because they had no homes in Boston, were carried to meet the other hearses in King Street, near the scene of the shootings. A long procession then followed the black carriages to the cemetery, where the victims were buried in one grave.

John Adams was to write of the Boston Massacre years later, "On that night, the foundations of American independence were laid."

But though they could not foresee this future, patriot leaders who were trying to stir up trouble for the British made sure that the deaths of the five men were not forgotten.

The *Boston Gazette* published an account of their deaths with black borders of mourning, with pictures of coffins, skulls, and crossbones.

Samuel Adams began to write of the clash between soldiers and civilians as the Boston Massacre, the name by which it is known to this day.

Paul Revere, the silversmith and engraver who was secretly working for the Revolution, copied a drawing of the massacre by a Boston artist and published it—one of the most famous engravings of American history. Thousands of copies were circulated throughout the colonies to create sympathy for the people of Boston and hatred of the British troops.

Captain Preston and several of his soldiers were tried in Boston. The captain was found not guilty since the court ruled that he had acted to protect his troops. Two soldiers who were found guilty were branded in the hand with a hot iron. This did not satisfy the patriot leaders.

Three years later, John Adams called on the memory of the victims of the Boston Massacre to help cause an open break between America and England.

Adams sent Governor Hutchinson a letter that would not be forgotten, a letter that he pretended had been written by a dead man. It was actually meant for use in newspapers:

Sir

You will hear from Us with Astonishment. You ought to hear from Us with Horror. You are chargeable before God and Man, with our Blood.—The Soldiers were but passive Instruments . . . in our Destruction. . . . You were a free Agent. You acted, coolly, deliberately, with . . . Malice, not against Us in Particular but against the People in general, which in the Sight of the law is . . . Murder. You will hear from Us hereafter.

The signature in Adams's own hand was "Crispus Attucks."

It was to be many years later before the great orator Daniel Webster declared that the Boston Massacre was the turning point in the long struggle between England and her rebellious American colonists: "From that moment," Webster was to shout, "we may date the severance of the British Empire." The reckless bravery of Crispus Attucks had helped change the course of history.

4

The Master Spy of Yorktown

In the spring of 1781, General Washington rushed a band of 1,200 men southward to meet British raiders who were looting and burning their way through Virginia. The commander chosen for this tiny force was the Marquis de Lafayette, one of the youngest major generals in history. The Frenchman was determined to halt the invaders, who were led by the newest of British generals, the American traitor Benedict Arnold.

Lafayette, who was only twenty-three years old, had come to America four years earlier as a volunteer, sailing in a ship he had bought for the voyage. As one of the richest men in France, Lafayette had done much to bring help from King Louis XVI to the American rebels—troops, ships, guns, money, and uniforms. And in Virginia, at last, his dream had come true, a chance to command an American army, however small.

The young Frenchman soon found that his task was not easy. Virginia farmers hid their horses and wagons so that Lafayette's soldiers could not seize them for use against the enemy. The little army was often hungry, for people of the countryside refused to sell their meat and grain in exchange for the almost worthless American paper money. It was just as Governor Thomas Jefferson had warned Lafayette; Virginia was a state of "mild laws and a people not used to prompt obedience."

Lafayette also found that the enemy was too strong for him, since there were two British armies in Virginia, one under Benedict Arnold and another under Lord Charles Cornwallis. With better trained troops and thousands of horses stolen from Virginia plantations, the redcoats moved swiftly. The British burned the capital at Richmond, many warehouses full of valuable tobacco and supplies of rebel arms and food, and chased the Virginia legislature across the state. Governor Jefferson narrowly escaped capture and resigned his office. Lafayette complained to Washington, "I am not strong enough to get beaten. Government in this state has no energy and laws have no force. . . . The enemy can overrun the country."

Still, the Frenchman refused to give up. His troops hung about the British, as closely as they

The Marquis de Lafayette at Yorktown, by Jean-Baptiste Le Paon, 1783.
Perhaps James Armistead Lafayette, master spy and friend of the French
general, was the inspiration for the impressive figure in the background.

(The Kirby Collection of Historical Paintings,
Lafayette College, Easton, Pennsylvania)

American revolutionaries, black and white, fought British troops on
Bunker Hill in Massachusetts. Engraving after the painting by
Alonzo Chappel. *(The Chicago Historical Society)*

James Armistead Lafayette,
painted in later years
in military dress
by John B. Martin
*(The Valentine Museum,
Richmond, Virginia)*

Lord Dunmore, Governor General
of Virginia, issued this proclamation
promising freedom to all slaves
and indentured servants who
enlisted with the British army.
(Virginia State Library)

By His Excellency the Right Honorable JOHN Earl of DUNMORE,
Majesty's Lieutenant and Governor General of the Colony and Dominion of
Virginia, and Vice Admiral of the same.

A PROCLAMATION

AS I have ever entertained Hopes, that an Accommodation might have
taken Place between Great-Britain and this Colony, without being
compelled by my Duty to this most disagreeable but now absolutely necessary
Step, rendered so by a Body of armed Men unlawfully assembled, firing on His
Majesty's Tenders, and the formation of an Army, and that Army now on
their March to attack His Majesty's Troops and destroy the well disposed Subjects of this Colony. To defeat such treasonable Purposes, and that all such
Traitors, and their Abettors, may be brought to Justice, and that the Peace, and
good Order of this Colony may be again restored, which the ordinary Course
of the Civil Law is unable to effect; I have thought fit to issue this my Proclamation, hereby declaring, that until the aforesaid good Purposes can be obtained, I do in Virtue of the Power and Authority to ME given, by His Majesty; determine to execute Martial Law, and cause the same to be executed
throughout this Colony: and to the end that Peace and good Order may the
sooner be effected, I do require every Person capable of bearing Arms, to resort
to His Majesty's STANDARD, or be looked upon as Traitors to His
Majesty's Crown and Government, and thereby become liable to the Penalty
the Law inflicts upon such Offences; such as forfeiture of Life, confiscation of
Lands, &c. &c. And I do hereby further declare all indented Servants, Negroes,
or others, (appertaining to Rebels,) free that are able and willing to bear Arms,
they joining His Majesty's Troops as soon as may be, for the more speedily
reducing this Colony to a proper Sense of their Duty, to His Majesty's
Crown and Dignity. I do further order, and require, all His Majesty's Liege
Subjects, to retain their Quitrents, or any other Taxes due or that may become
due, in their own Custody, till such Time as Peace may be again restored to this
at present most unhappy Country, or demanded of them for their former sala-
tary Purposes, by Officers properly authorized to receive the same.

GIVEN under my Hand on board the Ship WILLIAM, off Norfolk,
the 7th Day of November, in the sixteenth Year of His Majesty's Reign.

DUNMORE.

(GOD save the KING.)

Agrippa Hull fought for six years with the Continental army, four of them with General Taddeus Kosciusko, the Polish patriot. Unidentified artist, 1848.   *(Historical Room, Stockbridge Library, Massachusetts)*

By His Excellency

GEORGE WASHINGTON, Esq;

General and Commander in Chief of the Forces of the

United States of America.

THESE are to CERTIFY that the Bearer hereof
~~Oliver Cromwell Private~~
in the ~~Jersey Battalion~~ ~~Regiment~~, having faithfully served the United States ~~for Six Years~~
_____ and being inlisted for the War only, is
hereby DISCHARGED from the American Army.

GIVEN at HEAD-QUARTERS the *fifth*
day *June 1783*

G Washington

By His Excellency's
Command,

Trumbull Sec'y

REGISTERED in the Books
of the Regiment,

_____ Adjutant.

THE above *Oliver Cromwell Private*
has been honored with the BADGE of MERIT for *Six*
Years faithful Service.

John Appleton

PHILLIS WHEATLEY NEGRO SERVANT to M.ʳ JOHN WHEATLEY, of BOSTON.

Published according to Act of Parliament, Sept.ᵗ 1, 1773 by Arch.ᵈ Bell, Bookseller N.º 8 near the Saracens Head Aldgate.

(Opposite page, top left) Oliver Cromwell served for nearly seven years under Washington. His honorable discharge, written in General Washington's own hand, was a treasured possession.

(The National Archives)

(Opposite page, top right) This engraving appeared in *The Colored Patriots of the American Revolution*, written by pioneer black historian William C. Nell in 1855. Top figure is a black artilleryman, and the bottom is Peter Salem, a hero of the Battle of Bunker Hill.

(American History Division, The New York Public Library, Astor, Lenox and Tilden Foundations)

(Opposite page, bottom) In 1845, William Ranney re-created the Battle of Cowpens, depicting a gallant black youth in the midst of the fighting.

(Courtesy of the State of South Carolina)

(Above) Frontispiece engraving (after Scipio Moorehead's portrait) of Phyllis Wheatley from *Poems on Various Subjects, Religious and Moral*, London, 1773.

(Library of Congress)

This is to certify that the Bearer by the Name of James Has done Essential Services to Me While I had the Honour to Command in this State. His Intelligence from the Enemy's Camp were Industriously Collected and more faithfully delivered He perfectly Acquitted Himself with some Important Commissions I gave him and Appears to me Entitled to every reward his Situation can Admit of. Done under My hand, Richmond November 21st 1784

Lafayette

The Marquis de Lafayette commended James Armistead Lafayette for his distinguished war record in this certificate dated November 21, 1784. Engraving with portrait after John B. Martin. *(Virginia Historical Society)*

The BLOODY MASSACRE perpetrated in King—street BOSTON on March 5th 1770 by a party of the 29th REGT

Paul Revere made this engraving of the Boston Massacre.

(The Colonial Williamsburg Foundation)

The identity of this
prosperous-looking black man
is lost, as were the identities
of so many black men and women
in American history.
Unidentified artist.
(The Historical Society of Pennsylvania)

Washington and his aide,
Billy Lee. Lee served
at the general's side
for the duration of the war.
(The Colonial Williamsburg Foundation)

Lt. Grosvenor and his Negro servant Peter Salem, painted by John
Trumbull in 1786. Salem fought bravely in several of the major battles
of the Revolution.   *(Yale University Art Gallery)*

Haitian revolutionary and king, Henri Christophe. Portrait by Richard Evans, ca. 1818.
(*Formerly in the collection of the late Sir Bruce S. Ingram, London; present whereabouts unknown*)

dared without risking battle. And since he could not hope to defeat the enemy openly, Lafayette began sending spies into the enemy camps.

The most important of the American spies was a black man, JAMES ARMISTEAD, the slave of William Armistead, a farmer who lived near the town of Williamsburg. He was only twenty-one, even younger than Lafayette, but the Frenchman saw that his volunteer was brave as well as bright and felt that he would be loyal to the American rebels— even though he had not been promised his freedom for risking his life as a spy.

James Armistead went at once to the camp of Benedict Arnold, made his way to headquarters, and sent Lafayette word of everything he saw. The British were not suspicious of the smiling young black man who had come as a volunteer and was so willing to serve officers in camp and to guide them on the roads. But messengers went out to Lafayette almost daily, reporting what Armistead had seen. Making use of these secret reports, a band of Virginia soldiers sneaked into the British camp one night and almost captured Benedict Arnold himself. Still the redcoats did not suspect young James Armistead. Arnold and his officers felt sure that the black man would remain loyal to them because he wanted most of all freedom from his life as a slave.

When Benedict Arnold left Virginia and returned to the war in the north, James Armistead went into the camp of Lord Cornwallis, where he served as a waiter at headquarters. He continued to report to Lafayette almost daily, though the risk of death was now greater and his work was much harder. Cornwallis was a good general who was careful to see that his enemies had little chance to learn his plans.

As Lafayette reported, "His Lordship is so shy of his papers that my honest friend says he cannot get at them." The Frenchman further complained to Washington that he was forced "to guess at every possible whim of an enemy that flies with the wind and is not within the reach of spies." But though Lafayette admitted that he was "devilish afraid" of Cornwallis and was worried because his spies could not steal British maps and orders, he continued to camp very near the enemy, warned of every redcoat move by messengers from James Armistead. The armies trailed west through Virginia, and then back to the coast from the Blue Ridge Mountains, the British raiders leading, the Americans following stubbornly, a few miles in the rear. Cornwallis seldom realized that he was being followed, but Lafayette pretended that his tiny force was driving the

British before it, in hopes of keeping up the morale of Virginia civilians.

James Armistead left no record of his life in the enemy camp during these weeks, but since he spent much time in the tent of Lord Cornwallis, he was certainly a trusted servant. He probably stood near the general during meals, serving food and drink and listening to the talk of officers, pretending that he did not understand their plans, and certainly did not dream of revealing them to Lafayette and the Americans. But often, by day and night, James Armistead whispered what he had overheard to other black men in the camp, and within a few hours Lafayette had word of British plans.

In July, when Cornwallis's army had moved to the east and was camped in the small city of Portsmouth, near Chesapeake Bay, James Armistead reported that a fleet of sailing ships had come to anchor in the harbor, ready to carry British troops to a new post. Lafayette expected news that Cornwallis had sailed, but for weeks there was no change. The ships lay idle at anchor day after day, and enemy troops remained in their camp at Portsmouth. At last, in early August, there was a warning from James Armistead: Cornwallis had sailed, no one knew where. The army of redcoats had disappeared from Portsmouth.

Within a few days, Lafayette's scouts learned the enemy's secret. Cornwallis was unloading his troops at Yorktown, a small tobacco port on the York River, within sight of the broad Chesapeake. Lafayette and his Americans moved nearer, to Williamsburg, where they could keep watch. They saw that Cornwallis was in no hurry to build defenses about the village. The weather was hot, and only a few men worked at digging trenches. Lafayette reported the news to Washington, who was still in the north.

Sometime during these days James Armistead returned to Lafayette's camp and no doubt told the French officer that he had been sent there by Cornwallis himself—as a spy for the British!

There was soon exciting word from headquarters. General Washington wrote Lafayette that "news of very great importance" was on its way. The commander urged the Frenchman to hold Lord Cornwallis in Yorktown and to prevent his army from escaping. Lafayette guessed the truth: Washington and the French commander in America, Count Rochambeau, were marching south with their troops, and at the same time French fleets were sailing for the Chesapeake. Cornwallis was to be cut off by land and sea.

Meantime, only Lafayette's small army could hold Cornwallis in place.

Lafayette reported to Washington, "I hope you will find we have taken the best precautions to lessen his Lordship's chances to escape."

By early September the trap was closing on Cornwallis. A French fleet defeated British warships at sea just outside the Chesapeake, drove them back to their port in New York, and anchored in the bay. By the middle of the month, Washington and Rochambeau and the first of their soldiers reached Williamsburg, where Lafayette welcomed them. Two weeks later the American and French armies, led by Lafayette's small force, marched the few miles to Yorktown and surrounded the village.

The allied soldiers dug trenches, ever closer to the enemy. Huge French cannon were hauled into place and began firing in early October. By October 19, after only ten days of shelling, Cornwallis surrendered. His army marched out from the battered lines of Yorktown and laid down its arms. The battles of the Revolution were over. The broken-hearted Cornwallis himself did not ride out with his troops on the day of surrender, but remained in his headquarters in a cave beside the York River.

It was only two days later, when he had recovered, that Cornwallis left the village. In defeat he went to the headquarters of young Lafayette. The two generals were talking of the campaign, looking over their maps, when Cornwallis looked up to see the familiar face of James Armistead. The black spy wore an American uniform. The British general shook his head grimly, for it was only then that he realized that the volunteer who had served him so faithfully was in truth an American counterspy. The cunning and devotion of this young slave had played an important part in winning the final battle of the war.

One year after a treaty of peace had ended the war, Lafayette wrote a certificate praising the work of James Armistead as a spy:

This is to Certify that the Bearer By the Name of James Has done Essential Services to me While I Had the Honour to Command in this State. His Intelligences from the Enemy's Camp were Industriously Collected and More faithfully deliver'd. He properly Acquitted Himself with Some important Commissions I Gave Him and Appears to me Entitled to Every Reward his Situation Can Admit of. Done Under my Hand, Richmond November 21st 1784

Lafayette

Soon afterward, James Armistead sent this certificate to the General Assembly of Virginia and asked that he be declared a free man. In his petition he said that he had volunteered to help against the British: ". . . during the time of his serving the Marquis Lafayette he often at the peril of his life found means to frequent the British camp, by which means he kept open a channel of the most useful communications to the army of the state . . . of the most secret & important kind; the possession of which if discovered on him would have most certainly endangered the life of your petitioner . . ."

Even now Armistead said he would not demand his freedom unless his master, William Armistead, could be paid a reasonable price "for the loss of so valuable a workman."

The Virginia General Assembly agreed. The state paid Armistead a fair price, and James Armistead became a free man. From that time onward, he called himself James Lafayette.

By the year 1819, when he was growing old, James Lafayette had become "poor and unable to help himself." Once more he turned for help to the assembly, which voted him $60, a large sum for those days. He was also granted $40 a year for the rest of his life, a pension such as those paid to privates who had served in the army during the Revolution.

One of the great days in James Lafayette's life came in 1824, when he was sixty-four years old, and the aging Lafayette visited Richmond on his final tour of America. Great crowds lined the streets to see the French hero who had made possible American independence, and thousands watched as the Marquis greeted James Lafayette as an old comrade.

It was during this visit to Richmond that James Lafayette sat for his portrait, painted by the well-known artist John B. Martin. The portrait still hangs in a Virginia museum, showing the lean, erect black spy, dressed in a handsome military coat as a reminder of the days when he had won his own freedom and helped to win that of his country as well.

It is thought that the friendship and faithful service of James Armistead Lafayette caused the Marquis to become a leader in the movement to end slavery and to extend help to the black people of many nations.

At the close of the Revolution, Lafayette suggested to Washington a plan "which might greatly benefit the black part of mankind." He suggested that they purchase "a small estate where we may try the experiment to free the Negroes and use them only as tenants."

This led Lafayette to other efforts to outlaw slavery. In Paris, five years later, he helped to found a society of The Friends of the Blacks, and for the rest of his life he supported efforts to give equal rights to men of all races.

James Armistead Lafayette was the best-known black spy in the American army, but he was by no means the only one.

A slave by the name of SAUL MATTHEWS served also as a spy and guide in the British camp at Portsmouth. The white colonel Josiah Parker said of him that he "deserved the applause of his country" for his bravery. A Virginia historian reported that this slave of Thomas Matthews "brought back military secrets of such value to Colonel Parker that on the same night, serving as a guide, he led a party of Americans to the British garrison . . ." At another time, when Saul Matthews's master and other white Virginia soldiers had fled across the state border into North Carolina, Matthews was once more sent to spy on the enemy and returned with plans of British movements. Such distinguished officers as Baron von Steuben, Peter Muhlenberg, and General Nathanael Greene praised Matthews highly for his services.

Like James Armistead, he continued to work as

a slave after the war, but at last he too asked the legislature for help and was granted his "full liberty" for his "very many essential services . . . during the late war."

Others served in the same way, among them two slaves whose records included only their first names:

"*Antigua*: In March 1783 a slave by this name was lauded by the General Assembly of South Carolina for his skill in 'procuring information of the enemy's movements and designs.' He 'always executed the commissions with which he was entrusted with diligence and fidelity, and obtained very considerable and important information, from within the enemy's lines, frequently at the risk of his life.' To reward him, the assembly liberated his 'wife named Hagar, and her child.' " Antigua seems to have remained a slave all his life.

"*Quaco*: During the British occupation of Newport, Rhode Island, Quaco's Tory master sold him to a colonel in the king's army. Quaco fled to the Patriot lines with valuable information. In January 1782, the General Assembly of Rhode Island, saying 'the information he then gave rendered great and essential service to this state and the public in general,' declared Quaco free."

We will probably never learn more of the work of black spies during the Revolution, but it is certain that these secret services were so valuable that without them the struggle for the country's independence might have been lost.

5

Three Black Legions

When General John Sullivan of New Hampshire went off to join the American army at the opening of the Revolution, he told one of his slaves to prepare to ride with him. "We're going to fight for liberty," the general said.

The shrewd slave replied, "It would be a great satisfaction to me to know that I was fighting for my liberty as well, sir."

The argument of his black servant struck the general as so fair and reasonable that he gave him his freedom at once.

Perhaps it was not by accident that this happened in New England, where few of America's slaves lived—and where many white men believed in human liberty for blacks and whites as well. New England furnished the only predominantly black regiment in the American army.

The best known was formed in Rhode Island because that colony was unable to find enough white volunteers to fill its quota—and because many blacks wanted to fight in exchange for winning their own freedom from slavery. The Rhode Island legislature, saying that since "the wisest, the freest, and the bravest nations" had freed their slaves to fight in their armies, Rhode Island should do so. Every slave in the state who volunteered was declared "absolutely free" and was paid the wages of a regular soldier.

A regiment was formed under the white Colonel Christopher Greene, a cousin of General Nathanael Greene, who was second in command to Washington.

A well-known French author, the Marquis de Chastellux, who saw them in Connecticut in the winter of 1781, wrote in his journal, ". . . at the ferry-crossing I met with a detachment of the Rhode Island regiment. . . . The majority of the enlisted men are Negroes and mulattoes; . . . strong, robust men, and those I saw made a very good appearance."

Not long afterward, when Washington's victorious army paraded in review at Yorktown, Virginia, Baron von Closen of the French army wrote in admiration, ". . . three-quarters of the Rhode Island regiment consists of Negroes, and that regiment is the most neatly dressed, the best under arms, and the most precise in its maneuvres."

Soon after it was formed in 1778 the regiment fought in the battle of Newport, which General Lafayette called "the best fought action of the war." Six American brigades under command of General John Sullivan opposed a powerful army of British and German troops, and when the enemy advanced from Newport in great strength, the raw troops of the black regiment, with its ninety-five ex-slaves and thirty freedmen, were in the path of one of the most feared German regiments. The Germans were hired troops, expert riflemen and veteran bayonet fighters, who wore thick uniforms and tall leather hats and wore their hair in tarred pigtails. They charged the black Rhode Islanders again and again with their bayonets, hooting in a language the Americans did not understand. Each time the Germans were thrown back in their attempts to take an American fort. "They found large bodies of troops . . . chiefly wild-looking men in their shirt sleeves, and among them many Negroes."

As a white Rhode Island historian wrote, "The newly raised black regiment, under Col. Greene, distinguished itself by deeds of desperate valor. Posted behind a thicket in the valley, they three times drove back the Hessians who charged repeatedly down the hill . . ."

The day after the battle, the German colonel on this front asked for a transfer to New York "because he dared not lead his regiment again to battle, lest his men shoot him for having caused them so much loss."

General Sullivan announced proudly in his report on the battle of Newport that the black regiment was entitled to "a proper share of the Honours of the day."

The regiment fought on through the war as the years dragged by, winning praise for its hard fighting at Red Bank, New Jersey, and Points Bridge. The Rhode Islanders were still with Washington's army when the end came with the surrender of Lord Cornwallis at Yorktown. But the regiment's commander and many of his bravest men did not live to celebrate the final victory.

On May 13, 1781, when the British attacked American lines along the Groton River in Connecticut, the rebel defenders, including the Rhode Islanders, were driven back.

Colonel Christopher Greene, who refused to retreat, was cut down and killed by the redcoats—but the sharp bayonets and swords reached the commander only "through the bodies of his faithful guard of blacks, who hovered over him to protect him, and *every one of whom was killed*."

Near the close of the Revolution a company of Boston's black soldiers marched through the city's streets at a smart step and halted in front of the mansion of the white patriot leader John Hancock, on Beacon Street.

Hancock came out to salute the veterans and presented them with a silk flag that he had ordered for this company, the Bucks of America, who had fought through the long war. The handsome flag bore the picture of a pine tree, the symbol of American liberty, with a running buck deer, the emblem of the company. It also bore a scroll with the initials of John Hancock and George Washington and thirteen red stars on a field of blue, representing the thirteen colonies.

The flag was accepted by the company's black commander, Colonel Middleton. As he presented the flag to the Bucks, Hancock said it was offered as "a tribute to their courage and devotion throughout the struggle."

The Bucks then marched to a nearby town, where they were entertained with food and drink and disbanded. Despite the long service for which they were honored by Hancock, almost nothing is known today of the war record of the Bucks of America. In fact, the only name from its roster that has come down to us is that of Colonel Middleton. Hancock, who had been President of the Continental Congress, knew that the Bucks had done much to win American freedom, but at the time evidently no one felt it was important to write the history of their part in the war.

An early Boston historian who knew Colonel Middleton in his old age left a glimpse of the brave officer, who was still strong and active, well known in the city as a violinist and a horse-breaker.

One day the colonel defied a white mob during an annual celebration by Boston blacks for the end of the slave trade. This holiday on which blacks always poured onto the green lawns of the Common had been initially prompted by the blacks' refusal to celebrate the Fourth of July.

It had become a custom for white boys of Boston to 'rive the blacks from the Common during this ceremony, but though the celebrating crowd usually fled in terror, this day was different, thanks to Colonel Middleton. The blacks, angry at the breaking up of their festival, determined to resist, and many of them marched to the Common with arms.

This account was left to us by a woman who knew Colonel Middleton well: "Soon, terrified children and women ran down Belknap Street, pursued by white boys, who enjoyed their fright. The sounds of battle approached; clubs and brickbats were flying in all directions. At this crisis Col. Middleton opened his door, armed with a loaded musket, and, in a loud voice, shrieked death to the first white who should approach. Hundreds of human beings, white and black, were pouring down the street. . . . Col. Middleton's voice could be heard above every other, urging his party to turn and resist to the last. His appearance was terrific, his musket was levelled, ready to sacrifice the first white man that came within its range. The colored party, shamed by his reproaches, and fired by his example rallied. . . ."

The only reminder of Colonel Middleton and his company's long service in the army is the fine silk flag, which is now kept in the Massachusetts Historical Society, its fading colors a reminder of the long-gone day when Hancock passed them to the colonel.

Another band of black volunteers, from the distant French-owned island of Haiti, entered the war on the American side in 1779—about 550 soldiers who had enlisted in San Domingo.

These men, who sailed with a French fleet under command of the Count d'Estaing in September, 1779, were put ashore at Savannah, Georgia, with an army of about 3,000 white Frenchmen. The invaders hoped to drive a British army out of Savannah, with the help of an American force led by General Benjamin Lincoln.

But the redcoats were too strong. They fought from long lines of trenches and forts built by thousands of slaves from the Georgia countryside, black men who also mounted heavy cannon and served as guides for the British.

Other thousands of blacks might have fought for the Americans, but Georgia's white patriots feared to put muskets into the hands of their slaves (many of whom had run off to join the British, who organized black units themselves and urged all slaves to flee their masters) and refused to send them to join General Lincoln's army.

The little army of Americans and French stormed the trenches, aided by the black band from Haiti, but was driven back by heavy cannon fire that killed many men. When the attackers began retreating, the British charged from their defenses, determined to wipe out the invasion force.

In the French-American rear guard, however, were the black volunteers from Haiti, who stood firmly against the redcoats. Though many fell, the black brigade held its lines until General Lincoln's army and its French allies could escape. General Lincoln's cavalry commander, Count Casimir Pulaski, a nobleman who had come from Poland to help the Americans, was killed in this fierce fighting.

Among the blacks who fought before Savannah was a twelve-year-old boy, HENRI CHRISTOPHE, who was to become a famous general and king of Haiti more than thirty years later. It is uncertain whether Henri was a freeborn volunteer during the fight for Savannah or whether he won his freedom for his bravery in the battle—both tales were told of him.

In any case, young Henri was slightly wounded in the rear guard's stand against the British and returned home to San Domingo to recover. He rose rapidly in the Haitian army, led a rebellion against the French, and became general-in-chief. He was first named President of Haiti and, after a civil war had torn his country, was crowned king in 1811. Haiti prospered under King Henri, but when his people rebelled, after eight years of rule, because of cruelty to his people, the ruler killed himself.

Among other famous black soldiers from Haiti who fought as young men at Savannah were MARTIAL BESSE, who was made a general by the French, and JEAN-BAPTISTE MARS BELLEY, who became one of the leaders of Haiti, as Deputy of the Convention that governed the country for a time.

Almost twenty years after the battle of Savannah, when General Besse visited the United States on official business, he landed at Charleston, South Carolina, dressed in his commander's uniform— only to be told by white South Carolinians that he must put up a bond as required by the state for all incoming blacks. The bond was forgotten and the General was admitted only when the French consul in Charleston protested that General Besse was representing his government on official business and that he had been wounded at the siege of Savannah, fighting to help set America free.

Several other black units fought with the white patriot forces, but their records are lost or incomplete. In 1778, in the midst of the war, about 750 black soldiers were serving in fourteen American brigades that made up a small part of George Washington's armies. Many of them who volunteered did so without the promise of winning their freedom—though in the end thousands did become free because of their army service.

6

Whose War? Whose Liberty? Whose Death?

Today's historians can rescue only a few of the Revolution's black heroes from the shadows of the past. Thousands remain as invisible men who helped our nation, men who marched and fought, spied and scouted, sailed and served as pilots. Except for the few whose stories are told in these pages, these men are now almost as little known as those of the gangs of laborers who dug trenches, cleared roads, built bridges, and cleared swamps for Washington's armies.

In addition, thousands of black women played important roles in the war—most of them lost to history. Perhaps the best known is the poet Phyllis Wheatley, whose weapons were words. She wrote an ode in praise of Washington, who was so impressed by it that he invited her to his headquarters near Boston and received her as a celebrity.

Even those black men who left records behind

give us only glimpses of the parts they played in the struggle. Almost all of those who served in the army were privates, however brave, strong, or experienced they might have been. Many of them were listed without names.

Students of the Revolution find traces of these unknown men on every hand.

In the last months of the war, when Maryland called for ships to sail against enemy raiders, one white patriot said he would gladly send his schooner, but it would be "with a Negro Skipper, as no white man would go." The schooner's fearless black skipper is only one of many unknown seamen. General Washington once wrote, "I have granted a Warrant for the $1,000 promised the Negro Pilots." We know nothing else of these men.

In Virginia's war records is a letter, hardly more than a scrap of paper, signed by a Colonel George Muter, telling of a black man known only as JUPITER who saved four cannon during a British raid on Richmond and later delivered the guns safely to Colonel Muter.

When Chief Justice John Marshall wrote a biography of Washington, he described a skirmish after the battle of Cowpens, South Carolina, in which Colonel William Washington was about to be slashed by a British sword "when a waiter, too small to wield a sword, saved him by wounding the officer with a ball from a pistol." A well-known painting of the battle shows a young black boy shooting down the British officer and saving the life of General Washington's cousin, but the youngster's name is unknown.

Another example of brave black men who died forgotten is the crew of the schooner *Liberty*, which fought twenty battles against British ships during the war. Captain James Barron, the skipper of this small ship of the Virginia navy, later became a commodore, the highest ranking officer of the U.S. Navy.

Commodore Barron wrote of the many brave patriots who had sailed and fought with him on the *Liberty:* "Amongst these, I take pleasure in stating there were several coloured men, who, I think, in justice to their merits should not be forgotten. *Harry* (a slave, belonging to Captain John Cooper) was distinguished for his zeal and daring; *Cupid* (a slave of Mr. William Ballard) stood forth on all occasions as the champion of liberty, and discharged all his duties with a fidelity that made him a favorite of all the officers." The Commodore failed, however, to mention other black men of the crew of *Liberty*, who were forgotten.

Even these nameless men left their mark on

history. They left behind them children and grand-children who were proud of the heroic sacrifices of blacks during the Revolution—descendants who continued to protest until slavery had been outlawed and all Americans were free.

Soon after Crispus Attucks had been shot dead on the snowy street in Boston, several slaves in Massachusetts demanded that the government set them free. They tried to shame white patriots who spoke of "Liberty or Death" and declared that "all men were created equal."

In 1773 a number of slaves in Boston and other towns of the colony wrote to Governor Hutchinson, protesting that no matter how hard or how faithfully they worked, neither they nor their children nor their children's children could ever own anything. They must live like beasts: "We have no Property! We have no Wives! No Children! We have no City! No Country. . . ."

Soon afterward, the slaves of Massachusetts asked for one day a week so that they could work for themselves, save their money, and return to freedom in Africa. The Governor and the House refused to hear their pleas. These appeals, however, were among the first public calls from black men for the end of slavery in America; they were to grow louder and more emphatic during almost a century of protest.

(At the close of the Revolution, the Northern states would begin to free all slaves, though in the South black slavery was so important to the economy that few whites would think seriously of doing likewise.)

But though their appeals were refused, even in the Declaration of Independence, thousands of enslaved black men did fight for the liberty of their country as the Revolution wore on.

Some of our forefathers, white and black, honored these brave patriots more than a hundred years ago. They began with the first Crispus Attucks Day, which was celebrated in Boston seventy-five years after the Revolution, just before the opening of the Civil War, which was to end slavery in America. The white orator Wendell Phillips, the speaker of the day, reminded his audience that the famous writer Ralph Waldo Emerson had said that, though the first gun heard around the world had been fired at Lexington, it was the Boston Massacre that first gave Americans courage to resist:

Who set the example of the guns? Who taught the British soldier that he might be defeated? Who first dared look into his eyes? Those five men! The fifth of March was the baptism of blood. . . . I place, therefore, this Crispus Attucks in the foremost rank of the men that dared.

When we talk of courage he rises, with his dark face, in the clothes of the laborer, his head uncovered, his arm raised above him defying bayonets. . . . When the proper symbols are placed around the base of the statue of Washington, one corner will be filled by the colored men defying the British muskets.

Today's Americans, looking back across two hundred years of history, should give special honor to those black heroes who fought for the liberty of a white nation in the hope that their descendants would one day be free and respected as equals, for they were perhaps the bravest and most unselfish Americans of all.

As Harriet Beecher Stowe was to write of them almost a century after the close of the Revolution, "We are to reflect upon them as far more magnanimous . . . [inasmuch as they served] a nation which did not acknowledge them as citizens and equals, and in whose interests and prosperity they had less at stake. It was not for their own land they fought, not even for a land which had adopted them, but for a land which had enslaved them, and whose laws, even in freedom, oftener oppressed than protected. Bravery, under such circumstances, has a peculiar beauty and merit."

For Further Reading

Herbert Aptheker. *A Documentary History of the Negro People in the United States*. New York, 1962.

Sidney Kaplan. *The Black Presence in the Era of the American Revolution, 1770–1800*. New York, 1973.

William C. Nell. *The Colored Patriots of the American Revolution*. Boston, 1855.

Benjamin Quarles. *The Negro in the American Revolution*. Chapel Hill, North Carolina, 1967.

Benjamin Quarles and Leslie H. Fishell, Jr. *The Black American*. Glenview, Illinois, 1970.

Joseph T. Wilson. *The Black Phalanx, A History of the Negro Soldiers of the United States*. Hartford, Connecticut, 1888.

Carter G. Woodson. *The Negro in Our History*. Washington, D.C., 1962.

Index

Have you read these ODYSSEY paperbacks?

ODYSSEY CLASSICS

L. M. Boston
THE CHILDREN OF GREEN KNOWE
TREASURE OF GREEN KNOWE
THE RIVER AT GREEN KNOWE
A STRANGER AT GREEN KNOWE
AN ENEMY AT GREEN KNOWE

Edward Eager
HALF MAGIC
KNIGHT'S CASTLE
MAGIC BY THE LAKE
MAGIC OR NOT?
SEVEN-DAY MAGIC
THE TIME GARDEN
THE WELL-WISHERS

Elizabeth Enright
GONE-AWAY LAKE
RETURN TO GONE-AWAY

Eleanor Estes
GINGER PYE
THE WITCH FAMILY

Carolyn Haywood
"B" IS FOR BETSY
BETSY AND BILLY
BACK TO SCHOOL WITH BETSY
BETSY AND THE BOYS

Anne Holm
NORTH TO FREEDOM

Carol Kendall
THE GAMMAGE CUP

Eleanor Frances Lattimore
LITTLE PEAR
LITTLE PEAR AND HIS FRIENDS

Mary Norton
BED-KNOB AND BROOMSTICK
THE BORROWERS
THE BORROWERS AFIELD
THE BORROWERS AFLOAT
THE BORROWERS ALOFT
THE BORROWERS AVENGED

Carl Sandburg
PRAIRIE-TOWN BOY
ROOTABAGA STORIES, PART ONE
ROOTABAGA STORIES, PART TWO

Virginia Sorensen
MIRACLES ON MAPLE HILL

William O. Steele
THE BUFFALO KNIFE
FLAMING ARROWS
THE PERILOUS ROAD
WINTER DANGER

John R. Tunis
THE KID FROM TOMKINSVILLE
WORLD SERIES
KEYSTONE KIDS
ROOKIE OF THE YEAR
YEA! WILDCATS!
A CITY FOR LINCOLN
IRON DUKE
THE DUKE DECIDES
ALL-AMERICAN
CHAMPION'S CHOICE

Henry Winterfeld
CASTAWAY IN LILLIPUT
DETECTIVES IN TOGAS
MYSTERY OF THE ROMAN RANSOM
TROUBLE AT TIMPETILL

Milton Meltzer
UNDERGROUND MAN

Turn the page for more Odyssey titles and ordering information.

ODYSSEY BOOKS

Burke Davis
BLACK HEROES OF THE AMERICAN REVOLUTION

Louis Haber
BLACK PIONEERS OF SCIENCE AND INVENTION

Virginia Hamilton
A WHITE ROMANCE
JUSTICE AND HER BROTHERS
DUSTLAND
THE GATHERING

Gary Soto
BASEBALL IN APRIL AND OTHER STORIES

Theodore Taylor
AIR RAID—PEARL HARBOR!

Paul Robert Walker
PRIDE OF PUERTO RICO

ODYSSEY/GREAT EPISODES

Kristiana Gregory
JENNY OF THE TETONS
THE LEGEND OF JIMMY SPOON

Dorothea Jensen
THE RIDDLE OF PENNCROFT FARM

Seymour Reit
BEHIND REBEL LINES

Look for Odyssey paperbacks in your local bookstore.
To order directly from Harcourt Brace, call 1-800-543-1918